Great Altar of Zeus

Bouleuterion

Hill of Kronos

Zanes

Treasuries

Stadium

Hippodrome

THE ANCIENT
GREEK
OLYMPICS

Richard Woff

OXFORD
UNIVERSITY PRESS

Richard Woff was a teacher and then a lecturer in education at the University of London. He is now Deputy Head of Education at the British Museum, where he organizes the Museum's provision for young visitors. Richard is well past winning an Olympic medal, but he does cycle to work sometimes.

With thanks to Judith Swaddling and Sam Moorhead.

© 1999 The Trustees of the British Museum

Published in the United States of America by
Oxford University Press, Inc.
198 Madison Avenue, New York, New York 10016
www.oup.com

Oxford is a registered trademark of Oxford University Press, Inc.

ISBN 0-19-521581-8

First published in 1999 by British Museum Press,
A division of The British Museum Company Limited,
46 Bloomsbury Street, London WC1B 3QQ

Designed and typeset in Swift and Formata by Jeffery Design
Printed in Slovenia

Illustration acknowledgements

© Allard Pierson Museum, Amsterdam 27 right

© Allsport 9 below left; 31 below left; 31 centre right;
Allsport/Al Bello 22 centre right;
Allsport/Nathan Bilow 24 below right;
Allsport/Shaun Botterill 21 below centre;
Allsport/Mike Cooper 31 below right;
Allsport/Tony Duffy 14 below right; 27 centre;
Allsport/Stephen Dunn 25 top right;
Allsport/Stu Forster 19 below right;
Allsport/John Gichigi 18 top;
Allsport/Mike Hewitt 17 below right;
Allsport/Doug Pensinger 27 below;
Allsport/Mike Powell 7 top left; 14 below left, below centre;
Allsport/Steve Powell 11 top left;
Allsport/Pascal Rondeau 13 below right; 21 below right;
Allsport/Ezra O. Shaw 25 below left;
Allsport/Nick Wilson 5 below right

© Armeefotodienst CH-3003 Bern 23 below

Susan Bird: 11 and 15 illustrations.

© The British Museum: 1; 4 top; 5 centre; 7 centre left, below left, top right; 10; 11 below; 12; 13 top, centre; 14 centre left, top right, centre right; 15 all photographs; 16; 17 below left, top right; 19 centre left, centre below; 21 top left; centre right; 22 below left, top right, below right; 23 left, top right, centre right; 24 left, top right; 25 top left, below right; 26 top right; 29; 30.

C.I.O./Collections du Musée Olympique 31 top left

Institute of Classical Studies, 28 below left, below centre, below right

Sam Kirby, © The British Museum 28 map artwork

Metropolitan Museum of Art, Rogers Fund, 1914. (14.130.12) 18 below

Sam Moorhead 28 top left

Prof. Dr. H. Mussche 6 below left; 11 centre left

Musées Royaux d'Art et d'Histoire, Brussels 6 right

© National Gallery, London. Degas, 'Young Spartans Exercising', 26 below left

Soprintendenza Archeologica per la Toscana – Firenze 4 below.

Staatliche Antikensammlungen und Glyptothek, Munich 20, 27 left

TAPS, Ministry of Archaeological Receipts Fund, Athens 8 below, 9 top left

Richard Woff 9 top right; 19 top left; 26 below right

Contents

How the Olympics began 4

Getting ready 6

The crowds gather 8

Day 1 10

Day 2 12

Day 3 16

Day 4 20

Day 5 24

Women and athletics 26

Games elsewhere in Greece 28

The end of the Olympics ... and a new beginning 30

Other books on the ancient Greeks and athletics 32

Index 32

How the Olympics began

Los Angeles! Paris! Tokyo! London! Barcelona! Sydney 2000! When we think of the Olympic Games, we think of the great cities of the world. But the ancient Olympics did not take place in a city, a town or even a village. The home of the ancient Olympics was Olympia, near the west coast of Greece. And nobody really lived there at all. Olympia was only important because it was sacred to Zeus, the king of the gods. It was in his honour that the Games were held.

This is a model of ancient Olympia. You can see clearly the wooded Hill of Kronos where Zeus wrestled his father.

The scene on this pot shows the funeral games for the dead hero Patroklos. Beyond the horses you can see one of the prizes: a tripod made of bronze. Above the chariot race, some heroes are hunting a fierce boar with javelins. The white figure is Atalanta, the great woman hero (see page 27).

We do not know how or when the Games began. Some stories tell us that Zeus himself started the Games. According to these stories, it was at Olympia that Zeus wrestled with his father Kronos for control of the world and arranged a set of contests for the gods to celebrate his victory. The poet Pindar says that Herakles held the first Games to celebrate finishing one of his Labours: he had diverted the river Alpheios to clean out the filthy stables of King Augeas, who lived nearby. In other stories a different Herakles, who helped protect Zeus when he was a baby, held a race there for his four brothers and awarded the winner a crown of wild olive leaves.

The goddess Athena leads Herakles to Mount Olympos to become a god. You can see the hero's club and lion skin. Herakles and all the other famous ancient Olympic athletes were men. Women were not allowed to compete at the games (see pages 26-27).

At Olympia was the ancient tomb of Pelops, a local hero who won an important chariot race. This may give us a clue as to how the Games began. To the ancient Greeks, heroes were not just famous people. The Greeks believed that long ago there had been a race of men who were so strong and brave that they were like the gods themselves. When a hero died, his relatives and friends held competitions, such as running, wrestling, and chariot racing as part of the funeral. Often the place where the hero was buried became sacred to the local inhabitants, who made sacrifices or other offerings to secure the hero's goodwill.

This also helps us to understand why Herakles is mentioned as the founder of the Olympic Games. Herakles was the son of Zeus and by far the greatest of the heroes. Apart from his famous 12 Labours, which included wrestling a lion and a bull, catching a deer and a wild boar, and holding up the sky, Herakles carried out many other feats of strength and speed. When he died, he was reunited with his father and so was the only hero who really became a god.

The original Games seem to have fallen into disuse. Later, perhaps in the ninth century BC, King Iphitos of Elis, the nearest town, was told by the oracle of Delphi that he could save Greece from plague and civil war by re-starting the Games. He established a truce and invited all the states of Greece to come together in peace to compete at Olympia. The ancient Greeks started to number the Games from 776 BC. The first Games consisted of one running race, the *stade* race, which was won by a local athlete named Koroibos. From this single race grew the greatest athletics competition in the world.

This is the new stadium being built for the Olympics in Sydney, Australia, in the year 2000.

Getting ready

Athletes needed to be at peak fitness for Olympia, so good training was vital. In ancient Greece, physical training was not just important for athletic competitions: men, who might have to fight in war, always had to be fit. All Greek cities had training areas where men could exercise. The two sorts of training area were the *palaistra*, where they trained for the combat sports, wrestling and boxing, and the larger *gymnasium*, for running and throwing events. Both looked similar: a rectangular space surrounded by covered colonnades for training in bad weather and for spectators.

Most athletes had trainers to prepare them and to advise them about exercise, hygiene and diet. Trainers knew, for example, that a high-protein diet of cheese and meat would help wrestlers to build up muscle. Trainers were experts in their sports. Ikkos from Tarentum, in southern Italy, was a former Olympic pentathlon champion and wrote a book on athletics training. Trainers observed the athletes carefully and suggested how they could improve their style and technique. A wrestling trainer might get one wrestler to use a hold on his sparring partner and then explain to the partner how he could counter it.

Olympic athletes had to be in training for the Games for 10 months. They and their trainers were required to swear an oath about this at the start of the Games. For the final month of training the competitors had to go to Elis, so that the organizers of the Games, the Hellanodikai, could supervise them and make sure they were up to standard. The word "Hellanodikai" means "judges of the Greeks".

This is the palaistra at Olympia today. The space between the columns and walls originally had a roof.

This wrestler is clearing the wrestling pit of rocks and breaking up the earth to make it softer. You can see the cap he wears to protect his ears during a fight.

This modern athlete is doing fitness training.

There were some training facilities at Olympia itself. The gymnasium was very large. It had a covered running track down one side that was the same length as the actual stadium. Nearby was the palaistra, which also had rooms around where athletes could oil their bodies, wash and bathe.

An athlete stands under the colonnade of a palaistra – you can see the tiles on the roof. He holds his boxing thongs in one hand and a palm branch of victory in the other. On the left is a statue of Hermes, the patron god of wrestlers.

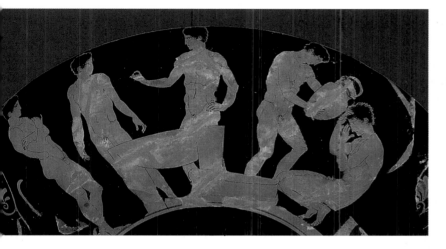

The ancient Greeks knew that cleanliness was an important part of being fit and healthy.

All athletes trained and competed naked. They coated their bodies in oil and then rubbed on sand, which stuck to the oil. Ancient Greek experts explain that this was for health reasons: some types of sand cleared the pores of the skin, others nourished it. The sand and oil helped the body stay cool in the summer and warm in the winter and protected against sunburn. After exercise, the athletes scraped off the sand and oil with a scraper called a *strigil* and then bathed.

Athletes carried their oil in small containers like this one – called an *aryballos* – and scraped it off with curved scrapers or strigils.

Athletes also needed ways of relaxing. Olympia had the only swimming pool in ancient Greece, although there were no swimming races. Archaeologists also think they have found a bowling alley in the palaistra.

It took time to organize the Games. The Hellanodikai started their detailed planning well in advance. The sacred area, which was called the *Altis*, had to look its best. The stadium and facilities were not used between sets of Games, so there was also a lot of clearing, cleaning and resurfacing to do before the festival.

Promachos was training for the Olympics when his trainer noticed that he had fallen in love and asked him about it. Promachos blushed. His trainer said, "I am not trying to embarrass you, I am just interested in your love affairs. I will go and talk to the girl." The trainer did not really talk to her, but came back with the following message: "She says that she will not refuse your love if you win at Olympia." This was just what Promachos needed and he won not just any victory, but beat the champion himself.

The crowds gather

The Olympics took place every four years in August. The local town of Elis had the responsibility for organizing them. In the spring of an Olympic year, three heralds set off from Elis. They wore wreaths of olive leaves and carried staffs. They travelled all over the Greek world, announcing the Olympic truce. The truce allowed competitors to travel safely to Olympia without fear of being attacked by robbers or by soldiers at war.

As August approached, tens of thousands of Greeks began to converge on Olympia. By this time of year the harvests were over and there was little work to do in the fields, so people had more leisure time. They came from towns nearby, from the cities of Athens, Sparta and Corinth, from all over mainland Greece, from the Greek islands and colonies in the eastern Mediterranean, and from the fabulously wealthy Greek cities of Sicily and southern Italy.

Some spectators and contestants reached Olympia by ship along the river Alpheios. Floods from the Alpheios buried the remains of Olympia in mud until they were rediscovered in 1766.

These spectators at a chariot race are lucky – they have proper seats. At Olympia only the priests, judges and most important guests had seats. The other 40,000 spectators had to sit or stand on the grassy slopes surrounding the stadium. There were no sunshades to protect the audience from the fierce August sun.

The stadium had water channels around it and basins from which spectators and competitors could drink.

Along with the spectators arrived merchants, food-sellers and people selling offerings to dedicate to Zeus. There were singers, musicians, poets, painters and entertainers of all kinds. The great festival was an opportunity to make money and to become well known. There were no hotels or guest houses and no Olympic village for the competitors. Everyone had to make his own arrangements. The princes and nobles had fine pavilions erected for them. Others brought simpler tents and shelters. Many simply spent the warm summer nights out in the open.

For all the competitors and spectators, rich or poor, the Olympics were more than just sport: they were part of the worship of Zeus. The ancient Greeks thought their gods were like humans. They needed food and drink, they could be kind or angry, they argued, they fought and they loved. They even looked like humans. However, they were vastly more powerful and fearsome. If a god or goddess wanted to appear to a human, he or she had to take on some sort of disguise. The mere sight of the body of a god could destroy a human being.

At an athletics contest, the fittest and strongest of the Greeks ran, threw and fought. By doing this, they were offering or sacrificing to the gods their speed, strength and power. Also, from those superbly fit bodies with their tightened muscles, their graceful movements and their bursts of explosive strength, the spectators could get a faint idea of what the awesome gods must be like.

The ancient Greek writer Plutarch tells this story: "Once, during the Games at Olympia, an old man wanted to watch, but could not find anywhere to sit. He worked his way around the whole stadium, but nobody was willing to make space for him. When at last he reached the part of the stadium where the Spartans were sitting, all the young men and many older ones too stood up to offer him their places. Immediately the crowd cheered. As he sat down, the old man shook his head sadly and said, 'It is such a tragedy that all the Greeks know what is right, but only the Spartans do it.'"

DAY 1

Programme

Morning	▶ Swearing-in ceremony
	▶ Boys' contests
	▶ Public and private prayers
Afternoon	▶ Speeches and recitals
	▶ Sightseeing tours
	▶ Reunions

You can see logs and flames at the top of this altar.

The festival was ready to begin. Soon the athletes would discover whether the training and special diets, the pain, the exhaustion and aching limbs would be worth it. They all knew that there were only winners at Olympia; you got nothing for second or third place.

The competitors and their fathers, brothers and trainers made their way to the *Bouleuterion* or Council Building of Olympia. There the 10 Hellanodikai were waiting for them. It was time to swear the Olympic oath. In the Bouleuterion was a statue of Zeus Horkios (Enforcer of Oaths). He held a terrifying thunderbolt in each hand. Over the cut-up flesh of a boar, they all swore that they had been in training for 10 months and that they would observe the rules of the Games. Then the Hellanodikai swore that they would be fair judges of the contestants.

As soon as he had sworn the oath, an athlete could go to one of the many altars in the sacred area, the Altis. There he sacrificed an animal and made burnt offerings to a god – to Zeus or Hermes, Apollo or Herakles – and prayed for victory. He might also ask a religious expert to examine the entrails of the sacrificed animal to look for any signs of victory hidden there.

The Olympic flame and symbol are modern inventions.

The only competitions on the first day were the running, wrestling and boxing for boys. The age-limit for entry was 12 to 18 years – but it was not possible to check the ages of contestants. There is a story that the judges thought one boy boxer looked too old, so they made him enter the men's event, which he won.

The afternoon was free, so the contestants could meet friends or go sightseeing. There were glorious things to see at Olympia. The Altis was full of statues of gods and goddesses and of previous winners in the Games. There was a row of buildings erected by Greek cities, where they kept the valuables they had given as offerings to Zeus. The temple of Hera was surrounded by 40 columns, no two of them the same. Inside was a wooden chest on which were carved pictures of gods and of heroes including Herakles and Pelops.

To remind the competitors of their oath, on the way into the stadium there was a row of 16 bronze statues of Zeus, called *zanes*. These were paid for with the fines from athletes who had been caught cheating. The arch is the entrance to the stadium.

This man may be one of the Hellanodikai (judges). You can see a finishing post behind him.

The statue of Zeus was one of the Seven Wonders of the World. It was 13 metres (43 feet) high. If Zeus had stood up, he would have taken off the roof of the temple!

The greatest sight of all was the enormous temple of Zeus. It had 34 gigantic columns. The whole temple shone with bright white plaster and in places was painted with patterns in red, blue and gold. The triangular pediments of the roof were filled with marble statues. The pediment at the eastern end showed Zeus watching over Pelops at the start of his chariot race. Above the doors of the temple were marble slabs carved with the 12 Labours of Herakles. But the most magnificent sight of all was inside the temple: the gigantic gold and ivory statue of Zeus himself.

That night the competitors went to their pavilions, tents or huts or lay back gazing up at the stars, their minds full of the excitement of the day and their stomachs fluttering at the thought of what the next four days would bring.

DAY 2

Programme

Morning	▶ Procession into the hippodrome
	▶ Chariot races
	▶ Horse races
Afternoon	▶ The pentathlon
Evening	▶ Parade of winners
	▶ Singing of victory hymns
	▶ Feasts and revels

The crowds woke early on the second day of the games. They jostled into position to see the opening spectacle of the second day: the procession of horses, riders and chariots into the *hippodrome*. The jangle of harnesses, the tossing manes and whinnying of the horses all added to the atmosphere of nervous tension.

The starting gates in the hippodrome.

Hippodrome means "horse-track" in Greek. The hippodrome was not a building but a large stretch of level ground with a raised bank or hill where spectators stood. Only the judges had seats! The racetrack was a large oval. At Olympia each lap was about 1,200 metres (three-quarters of a mile). The turns were marked by pillars. On top of the pillars were bronze statues of Pelops, victor in the original chariot race at Olympia, and of Hippodameia, his wife.

The chariot races were perhaps the most exciting – and dangerous – of all the events at Olympia. There were races for four-horse chariots and two-horse chariots.

The Greek playwright Sophokles wrote: "at the sound of the bronze trumpet off they started, all shouting to their horses and urging them on. The clatter of the rattling chariots filled the whole arena, and the dust flew up as they sped along in a dense mass. Each driver goaded his team to draw clear of the rival panting steeds, whose steaming breath and sweat drenched every flying wheel and bending back together."

The horse races were shorter than the chariot races – usually one circuit of the hippodrome. They took place after the chariot races on the same course.

By then the ground was churned-up and broken. Most jockeys were paid servants, although a few wealthy young men rode their own horses.

The races were very long by our modern standards – 4,000 metres (two-and-a-half miles) for young horses, up to 13,000 metres (eight miles) for the others. The tactic was to get ahead by the end of the straight and around the sharp turn safely ahead of the other chariots. Drivers who misjudged the turn or bumped another chariot could have a terrifying fall under the thundering hooves and wheels.

It was fashionable and popular for men to own horses, but good horses were very expensive, so only the richest people could afford to enter. This meant that winners in the chariot races could afford the greatest celebrations, the finest statues and the most beautiful victory hymns.

Alkibiades, a wealthy Athenian, tried to win the support of the people of Athens by reminding them of his achievements in chariot racing. In one Olympics his chariots had won first, second and third places in the chariot race.

In spite of their oaths, competitors did try to cheat. In 65 AD the Roman Emperor Nero bribed the judges. Nero was thrown from his chariot, but the judges stopped the race so he could remount. Nero then failed to complete the race. However, he was declared the winner on the grounds that he would have won if he had finished! After Nero's death his name was taken off the victor-lists and the bribe was paid back.

The jockeys rode bareback (saddles and stirrups had not been invented). It was a risky business for the riders – many fell off and were injured or even killed.

Chariot racing could be very dangerous – this chariot has crashed and horses and driver are tangled up.

DAY 2

In the afternoon the crowds moved over to the stadium for the pentathlon. In this competition the athletes took part in five different events:

discus
> **javelin**
>> **jumping**
>>> **running**
>>>> **wrestling.**

It was worth making a good start. If an athlete won the first three events of the five, the last two were cancelled.

In ancient times the discus was larger and heavier than it is today, about 2.5 kg (5.5 lb) in weight. It was made of bronze, lead or even marble. The flat, round shape has changed little. A set of official discuses was kept at Olympia to prevent cheating.

The current Olympic record for a discus throw is 69.4 metres (227.7 feet). We do not know what distances the throwers managed at Olympia because nobody kept a record of the distances. All that mattered was who won at each competition. There is also a lot of discussion among experts about whether or not the throwers were allowed to spin around before releasing the discus. If they were not allowed to, it is very unlikely that they would have come anywhere near the modern distances.

Javelin throwing is the Olympic event that has the closest connection with war. Warriors, especially those in the cavalry, could throw these deadly spears at the enemy without coming in range of their swords.

Exoidas dedicated this discus to the gods to commemorate his victory. You can see his name written backwards on the right at the bottom.

The Greek poet Homer wrote: "Then Odysseus leaped up and grabbed a discus far bigger and thicker than was usually used in competitions. He swung it round once and released it. The stone hummed on its way and the crowd ducked down as it hurtled through the air."

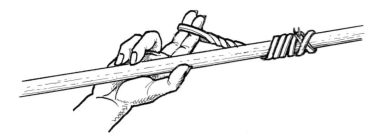

Today, Olympic athletes still take part in pentathlons, but some of the events are different. Do you know which ones? *(The answer is at the bottom of the page.)*

The javelins were about the height of a man. They were thrown in exactly the same way as they are today, with a run-up and a smooth overarm throw. However, ancient Greek athletes wrapped a strip of leather around the shaft of the javelin *(see the drawing above)*. The thong unwound as the javelin was thrown, spinning it so that it flew straighter.

There was no high jump in Greek athletic competitions, only the long jump.

Competitors also ran a sprint race of probably one length of the stadium. If there was no outright winner after the sprint, the remaining competitors took part in wrestling. You can read more about running and wrestling on pages 17–19 and 20–21.

This long-jumper looks as if he is going to win. The previous jumps are marked with pegs in the ground.

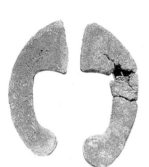

These jumping weights are made of lead.

We do not know for certain whether the jumpers took a run-up or did a standing jump. Pictures on pots show that they held heavy weights in their hands and swung them to help them jump. This is a very difficult technique; modern long-jumpers have tried it, but the weights tend to make them fall over when they land. The Greeks did record the lengths of two jumps and they were both further than 16 metres (52 feet). This is nearly twice the length of the current Olympic record, so some experts think that the Greeks used a multiple jump, like our modern triple jump – the Olympic record for triple jump is a little over 18 metres (60 feet).

Modern women athletes take part in the heptathlon (with seven events) and men in the two-day decathlon (with 10 events).

At the end of the day, the crowds gathered at the shrine of the hero Pelops, winner of the first chariot race at Olympia. There they re-enacted his funeral ceremonies. Afterwards, the winners paraded around the Altis and specially written hymns were sung in their honour. The first day of competition ended with feasts and celebrations. For some of the athletes, the Games were over. They either rejoiced in victory or were saddened by defeat. For others, the tests of their speed and strength were yet to come.

Answer: The modern pentathlon consists of horseriding, fencing, shooting, swimming and cross-country running.

DAY **3**

Programme

Morning	▶ Great procession to the Temple of Zeus
	▶ Official sacrifice to Zeus
Afternoon	▶ Running races
Evening	▶ Public banquet

The morning of the third day saw the most important religious event of the whole Olympic festival: the sacrifice to Zeus. All the competitors gathered at the entrance to the sacred Altis. There they were joined by ambassadors from the Greek states, who brought with them trays and large plates, mixing bowls for wine, jugs and drinking cups, all made from gold and silver. These were symbols of the wealth of their cities and would be used at a great banquet that evening. Attendants led 100 oxen, donated by the people of Elis. Finally, the 10 Hellanodikai arrived, dressed in their purple robes. The great procession was ready.

The huge temple of Zeus, which stood at the centre of the Altis.

Accompanied by cries of delight and wonder from the crowds, the procession moved off. It made its way around the Altis, passing the temple of Hera, the tomb of the hero Pelops, the temple of Rhea (mother of Zeus) and the treasure houses of Greek states from Sicily and Italy and elsewhere around the Mediterranean. Amidst the noise and bustle, the oxen strained on their halters, tossing their heads, and the attendants fought hard to control the animals.

The procession passed in front of the temple of Zeus. From deep inside the temple, through its open doors, the huge gold and ivory statue of the king of the gods gazed out. At last, they reached the great altar. The oxen were led forward and the priests cut their throats and let their life-blood flow out. Quickly, the attendants carved up the animals. Then the priests wrapped the thigh bones in fat and carried them to the top of the altar. There they burned the fat and bones and the smoke rose up to the gods. The rest of the meat was put to one side ready for the public banquet that evening.

How can you tell these athletes are running in the dolikhos and not in a sprint?
(The answer is at the foot of the page.)

In the afternoon, the runners got their chance at glory. The first race was the long-distance *dolikhos*, which was 20 or 24 lengths of the track, that is about 3,800 metres ($2^{1}/_{4}$ miles) or 4,600 metres ($2^{3}/_{4}$ miles). Unlike on a modern running track, there were no lanes or staggered starts. The bends were very tight – just a post at each end of the track – and athletes pushed and jostled for position. The turning posts provided opportunities for cheating by tripping or even by taking a short cut in the crowd of runners. It was a real advantage to take the lead early and to try to hold it to the end. The dolikhos was the longest race at the ancient Olympics: the marathon only became an event in modern times.

A sacrifice. The men on the right have wrapped meat around spits and are ready to roast it on the fire on the altar. The man on the left is pouring an offering of wine.

Like today, the most prestige came to the runner who won the short sprint, the *stade*. The stade was one length of the track, about 192 metres (630 feet). The winner of the stade race had the whole of that year's Games named after him. It was the most ancient event at the Olympics – in fact, for the first 50 years of their history, it was the only event. The last running race was the *diaulos*, which was two lengths of the track, about 385 metres (1,265 feet).

These runners are clearly sprinters. But what is unusual about the way they are running? *(Answer at the bottom of the page.)*

The ancient Greek poet Homer describes the funeral games held in honour of the dead hero Patroklos during the War of Troy. In the running race, the heroes Aias and Odysseus are battling it out for the lead: "As they came closer to the finish, Odysseus prayed to Athena, the bright-eyed goddess, and asked her to give speed to his feet. Athena heard his prayer and granted his wish. Just as the two swift heroes were about to reach the prizes at the end of the race, Aias slipped. Athena made this happen exactly where the ground was covered with cow dung from the cattle that had been sacrificed earlier that day. So Aias lay there with his mouth and nose full of cow dung, while Odysseus passed him, crossed the finishing line first and won the silver bowl."

Answer: They are leading with left arm and leg at the same time. You try running like that!

The starting line at Olympia, with grooves for the runners' toes.

All foot races finished at the western end of the stadium, with the winners always facing the sacred Altis. This meant that there had to be a starting line at both ends of the stadium for races with an odd and an even number of lengths.

The ancient runners did not use starting blocks or a crouching start. Instead, they made a standing start from stone slabs laid across the track with grooves carved in them so that they could grip with their bare toes. The starter used a blast from a herald's trumpet or a shout of *"apite"* – go! The penalty for a false start was worse than just being disqualified – you would be whipped!

Ancient runners were less specialized than nowadays and some competed in all three running events. If they won all three at the same Olympics, they were called triplers. One athlete, Leonidas, from the island of Rhodes, was a tripler at four successive Olympics: 164, 160, 156 and 152 BC.

In the evening, the great public banquet took place. Guests of honour dined in the Presidents' Hall, a special building reserved for entertaining important people. However, the Olympics were a celebration for everyone, so the athletes, their families and guests and all the spectators would receive a share of the meat from the morning's sacrifice. The public banquet was the opportunity for the representatives of the Greek cities to display their gold and silver tableware. Sometimes powerful and wealthy men got carried away with themselves. Alkibiades, a rich Athenian noble, dared to use the official gold and silver for his own private party!

A blast from a trumpet meant "Go!".

This was the starting position for any running race in the ancient Olympics.

Look at the way a modern runner gets maximum speed from the starting position, by crouching and using starting blocks.

19

DAY 4

Morning	▶ Wrestling
Midday	▶ Boxing and the pankration
Afternoon	▶ Running race in armour

On the fourth day of the Games, the spectators were filled with excitement as they made their way to the events. They chattered and called the names of their favourites. This was the day of the contact sports, the wrestling, boxing and pankration.

The bearded wrestler has the younger man in a double arm lock and forces his head down towards the ground.

Size and strength were the most important qualities of a wrestler. Small men had little chance of winning because there were no weight categories. Greek wrestlers used all sorts of holds, lifts and movements to try to bring their opponent down. Like the other athletes, wrestlers oiled their bodies before fighting, but then they covered themselves in powder so it was possible to get a grip. If an opponent's back or shoulders touched the ground, this was a "fall". Three falls won the fight. The oil made it easy to tell if there had been a fall, because the sandy earth on which the wrestlers fought stuck to their oily skin. Kleitomakhos was famous for going through a whole wrestling competition without once getting his shoulders sandy.

Wrestling was a tough sport. There were no rounds and competitors kept on fighting until one of them lost. There was even a law in Athens that said that a wrestler could not be prosecuted for accidentally killing an opponent. Fortunately only one wrestler, whose name was Telemakhos, ever killed his opponent, but he was not disqualified from the competition.

A trainer watches carefully as a wrestler completes a throw called the "flying mare".

In Greek myths, heroes were often especially good at wrestling. Peleus had to wrestle with a sea-goddess who kept changing form to try to escape from him. The hero who was best at wrestling was Herakles. Apart from wrestling a lion, Herakles also wrestled a giant who got his strength from the earth. Herakles only won by lifting the giant up until he lost all his power and died.

Herakles does the "flying mare" on a lion during his first Labour.

An ancient Greek writer describes a wrestler getting ready for a fight: "He shakes any excess powder off his body and stretches his arms out in front of him. He steadies himself on his feet, flexes his legs, bends his back and shoulders forward, tilts his neck up slightly, tenses his muscles and waits, motionless, eager to get to grips with his opponent."

DAY 4

At midday, when the sun was overhead and could not shine in anyone's eyes, the toughest of all the Olympic sports began: the boxing. Boxers were often cut and disfigured and there are stories of boxers being killed. There were no rounds, so fights could go on for hours until one man was either knocked unconscious or gave in. Once a fight went on so long that it was almost dark. The boxers decided simply to stand and exchange punches one at a time, without defence, until one of them won.

Boxers did not wear padded gloves like they do today. Early boxers wrapped strips of soft leather around their hands. After about 500 BC, they started wearing long gloves with thick ridges of stiff leather across the knuckles.

Boxers usually went for an opponent's head and face. Only in later times did they use their hands and arms for protection, so fast footwork was important to avoid punches. Even if a boxer could not avoid a punch, it was important not to appear to be hurt. A boxer named Eurydamos had his teeth smashed by a punch, but he quickly swallowed them so that his opponent would not notice.

You can see blood pouring out of the nose of the boxer on the left.

This boxer is using his teeth to help fasten his gloves.

The final combat event in the Olympics was the pankration, which means "all-strength" in Greek. This event combined boxing and wrestling, but also allowed wrestling on the ground, slapping, kicking, and using foot and leg holds and strangleholds. The only things that were not permitted were gouging and biting. The aim of the pankration was to make your opponent give in. He would indicate this by holding a finger up to the judge.

Most pankration fights started with the pankratiasts standing up, trying to get a grip. One famous pankratiast, called Sostratos, earned the nickname Mr Fingertips, because the first thing he did was to grasp his opponents' fingers and try to break them by bending them back. Usually, a pankration bout ended up on the ground as each fighter struggled to find a hold that would force the other into submission.

Although the pankration seems the most violent sport, the Greeks did not think it was as violent as boxing, but it was dangerous enough to have been won once by a dead man! Arrakhion's opponent was holding him in a scissors grip with his legs and was also trying to throttle him with his hands. Arrakhion grabbed the man's foot and broke one of his toes. The pain made the opponent give in, but just at that moment Arrakhion died from the throttling. The victory was still awarded to Arrakhion.

A bronze helmet and pair of greaves (leg armour): in the early days, runners in the hoplitodromos had to wear greaves.

Here are two pankratiasts fighting. The trainer is coming in with his stick because one of them is cheating. Can you tell what he is doing wrong? *(The answer is at the bottom of the page.)* You can also see two boxers – notice the cuts on the face of the right-hand one.

The final event in the ancient Olympic Games was the *hoplitodromos* (race in armour). This may seem strange to us, but to the ancient Greeks it made sense as it reminded them that one of the purposes of athletics was to prepare men to fight in battle. The competitors had to run two lengths of the stadium wearing helmets and carrying shields. We know that the number of entrants was limited to 25 because 25 identical shields were kept in the Temple of Zeus to make sure that no one could cheat by having a lighter shield than the others.

The hoplitodromos.

Every year the modern Swiss army holds a race in which the soldiers have to carry their guns and packs.

DAY **5**

Programme

Morning	▶ Procession of victors
	▶ Presentation of wreaths
Afternoon and evening	▶ Celebrations and banquets

All the events were over. The clashes of strength and fierceness in wrestling and boxing, the speed and stamina of the running, the power of the discus and javelin, the daring and determination of the chariot racing, all of these had reached their climax. The losers in the contests received nothing. Now was the moment for the winners.

The man at the front of the procession is announcing the victory. At the back, an attendant holds the crown of victory and the prize: a metal tripod.

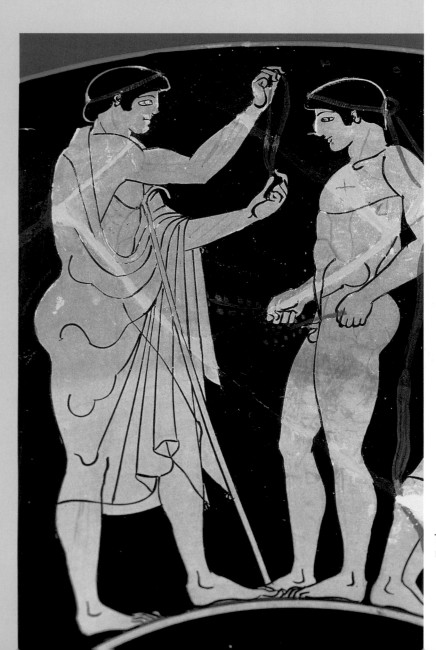

A modern medal ceremony.

This athlete has winner's ribbons tied around him.

Nike, the goddess of victory, crowns a winner.

For the last time, the spectators, trainers and athletes made their way in a procession to the Temple of Zeus. At their head walked the winners. Immediately after their contests, they had purple ribbons tied around their heads and limbs to mark them out. Now they were to receive the reward for which they had come to Olympia.

The procession made its way past an ancient wild olive tree sacred to Zeus. Just before the festival a boy was chosen whose parents were still both alive. For each event he cut a leafy branch from the tree using a golden sickle. The leaves were then woven into wreaths. When the procession reached the front of the temple, the winning athletes stepped forward. To the cheers of the crowds, the Hellanodikai placed a wreath of wild olive on the head of each winner. When all of them had been crowned, their fathers, brothers and friends rushed forward to congratulate them and the excited spectators hurled high into the air handfuls of leaves and flower petals, which drifted down on to the athletes in a shower of celebration.

A modern victory procession: the New York Yankees parade through Manhattan after winning the Baseball World Series in 1998.

A gold medal from the Olympics in Atlanta in 1996.

The rest of the day and the evening were spent in feasting. There was a huge public banquet as well as magnificent private parties that lasted well into the night. Competitors and their guests drank wine and sang hymns of victory as they strolled for one last time around the Altis, their heads and shoulders adorned with wreaths and garlands of flowers. They shared memories of the festival just past and dreamed of others to come. They looked forward to the victorious athlete's return home. He could expect a special reception, celebrations and feasts, large sums of money and other honours from his city, and a fine statue of himself in the market place.

A party.

If he could afford it, or if his city and friends could, the best reward of all was a statue in the sanctuary of Olympia itself. There were hundreds of statues of victorious athletes at Olympia. Each one reminded future generations that in that single moment of victory, a man had become like a god.

25

Women and athletics

Women were not allowed to compete in the Olympic Games. The exception was horse-owners, who could enter without actually being there. Only unmarried women were allowed to attend the Games. Ancient Greek girls married at about 13 years of age. One woman, who wanted to see her son compete, disguised herself as his trainer. When he won, she became so excited that she leapt up and her disguise was accidentally pulled off. From that day on, trainers as well as athletes had to attend the Games naked!

The goddess Hera, wife of Zeus, was a very important goddess at Olympia. Her temple was about 50 years older than that of Zeus. In honour of Hera, a running race for girls was held every four years in between Olympic Games. This was a sprint over the length of the stadium less one-sixth, that is about 160 metres (173 yards). The winner received a crown of wild olive, just like the male winners, and a painting of her was put up in the colonnade of Hera's temple.

This bronze girl is from Sparta. She hitches up her skirt so she can run better.

The Temple of Hera at Olympia.

Spartan boys and girls exercise together in this painting by the nineteenth-century French painter Edgar Degas.

Athletics were originally closely connected with war. As it was men who did the fighting, athletics were also closely connected with the whole idea of being and becoming a man. For this reason, there was usually no place for women in ancient Greek athletics. One exception was at Sparta, where exercise for girls was thought important so that they would be fit enough to give birth to healthy children, especially boys.

Atalanta wrestles with Peleus, the father of Achilles.

Women did play other physical games unconnected with athletics and, therefore, the role of men. They played games of skill such as knucklebones – a bit like our "jacks" – and a range of ball games. They also played a game called *ephedrismos*, which was like a combination of skittles, piggyback and blind man's buff!

In Greek myths, there was one great woman athlete. Her name was Atalanta. Her talent was running, but she also beat the father of the great warrior Achilles at wrestling. Atalanta was so close to being a man that she even accompanied the male heroes on a hunt to kill a huge and ferocious wild boar. Atalanta was finally beaten in a race by a man who then married her. But Atalanta was not a normal woman. When she was born her father, who wanted a son, had left her out in the wild to die. A bear had found her and brought her up. It was through stories like this that the ancient Greeks explored and found reasons for traditions such as excluding women from athletics.

Two young women playing ephedrismos.

Games elsewhere in Greece

The Olympics were the most famous athletics competitions in the ancient Greek world, but they were not the only ones. Four sets of games were called panhellenic or "all-Greek" games, because they were open to competitors from any Greek city in the world. These panhellenic games were the Olympic, the Pythian, the Isthmian and the Nemean Games.

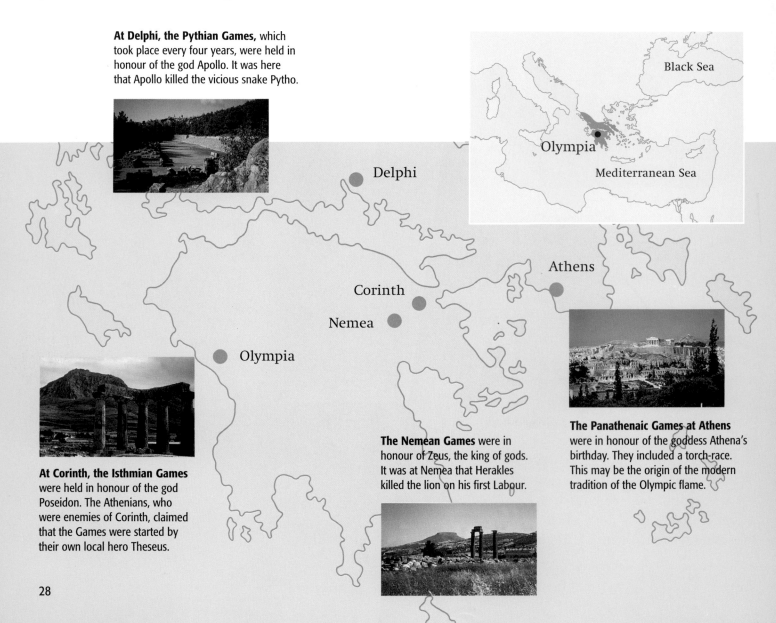

At Delphi, the Pythian Games, which took place every four years, were held in honour of the god Apollo. It was here that Apollo killed the vicious snake Pytho.

Black Sea

Olympia

Mediterranean Sea

Delphi

Athens

Corinth

Nemea

Olympia

At Corinth, the Isthmian Games were held in honour of the god Poseidon. The Athenians, who were enemies of Corinth, claimed that the Games were started by their own local hero Theseus.

The Nemean Games were in honour of Zeus, the king of gods. It was at Nemea that Herakles killed the lion on his first Labour.

The Panathenaic Games at Athens were in honour of the goddess Athena's birthday. They included a torch-race. This may be the origin of the modern tradition of the Olympic flame.

Individual Greek cities also arranged games, which were sometimes open only to the inhabitants of the city. The best known of these were the Panathenaic Games in Athens. After Alexander the Great spread Greek culture further east, many of the wealthy cities in what are now Turkey, Syria and Egypt set up games.

The prizes at the Panathenaic Games were large amphoras (storage jars) full of the finest olive oil. One side showed the goddess Athena with a helmet, shield and spear. The other side usually showed the event for which the prize had been awarded.

Athletes were now able to compete in games throughout the year, so it was possible for them to become full professionals. In the earliest days, only kings and nobles had been able to compete in contests. Keeping horses was expensive, so chariot and horse racing always remained the events of the super-rich, but professionalism meant that any man could become a famous athlete as long as he had the talent and opportunity.

In a book by the ancient Greek writer Lucian, one of the characters is asked "What are the rewards for athletics?" He answers: "At the Olympic Games, a crown of wild olive leaves, at the Isthmian, a crown of pine, at Nemea, a crown interwoven with wild parsley, at the Pythian games apples from the god's holy trees and finally, here at the Panathenaic Games, oil from the sacred olive."

In AD 97, Apollonios, a boxer from Alexandria in Egypt, lost his chance to compete at the Olympics. He arrived late for the final period of training, claiming that his voyage had been delayed by unfavourable winds. However, the Hellanodikai discovered that he had been too busy collecting his prize money from cities in Turkey, so they disqualified him.

This base from a statue shows the prizes won by an Athenian athlete. From left to right you can see a Panathenaic amphora, a wreath from the Isthmian Games, a shield from some games at Argos and another wreath. From the three letters that remain, can you work out where the athlete won the prize on the right-hand side? *(The answer is at the bottom of the page.)*

Answer: Nemea

The end of the Olympics.

The cement that held the Olympic Games together was the worship of Zeus. Even when other athletics competitions could offer larger prizes, the Olympics preserved the special connection with the king of the gods.

Gradually, this connection became weaker. In 336 BC Alexander the Great had gold and ivory statues of himself and his family set up at Olympia. These materials were usually used for statues of gods, so Alexander was suggesting that he could be identified with Zeus. Later, Roman emperors did similar things: Augustus had one of the temples at Olympia converted into a shrine to himself.

Over the years, generals plundered the riches of Olympia to finance wars. Its buildings were pulled down to build walls against foreign invaders. The Christian emperors of Rome banned the worship of non-Christian gods. Finally, the site was destroyed by invaders, earthquakes and floods. The last time the ancient Olympic Games were held was probably in the late fourth century AD. They had lasted for more than 1,100 years.

This drawing was made in 1806. You can see the Hill of Kronos on the left. The site of Olympia is still buried beneath the silt.

and a new beginning

Baron Pierre de Coubertin, the founder of the modern Olympic movement.

During the nineteenth century AD, French and then German archaeologists excavated Olympia. Their discoveries caught the imagination of a French nobleman, Baron Pierre de Coubertin. He thought that physical training was a way of building the strength and pride of young French people. He also believed that if athletes from around the world competed against each other, not for money, but for simple rewards, this would create greater international co-operation and friendship.

Coubertin devoted himself and most of his wealth to setting up a new Olympic competition. In 1896 the first modern Olympic Games were held in a new stadium in Athens. There were 42 events with 285 contestants, all of whom were men. Thirteen countries were represented: the United States and 12 European countries. One hundred years later, in 1996 at Atlanta, 10,768 men and women from 79 countries competed in 271 events.

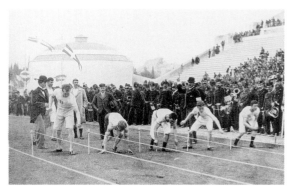

The start of the 100 metres at the first modern Olympics in Athens in 1896. Notice the mixture of ancient and modern starting positions.

Politics have always been part of the Olympics. In the fifth century BC, Elis sided with Athens in a war and banned Sparta from the Olympic Games. In Berlin in 1936, the African-American athlete Jesse Owens spoiled Adolf Hitler's racist plans. Hitler had intended that the Olympics would prove the superiority of the German people. Owens won three gold medals.

The closing ceremony of the centennial Olympics in Atlanta, Georgia, in 1996.

Other books on the ancient Greeks and athletics

British Museum Activity Book, The Ancient Greeks, British Museum Press, 1986.

Fleming, Fergus, *Greek Gazette,* Usborne, 1997.

Freeman, Charles, *Ancient Greeks,* Spotlights Series, S&S and Oxford University Press, 1996

Millard, A., Pocket Guide, *Ancient Greece,* Usborne, 1992.

Pearson, Anne, *Eyewitness Guide to Ancient Greece,* Dorling Kindersley, 1992.

Ross, Stewart, *The Original Olympic Games,* Wayland, 1998.

Shuter, Jane, *Ancient Greece Series,* Heinemann Library, 1999 (for young readers).

Swaddling, Judith, *The Ancient Olympic Games,* British Museum Press and University of Texas Press, second edition 1999 (for older readers and adults).

Index

Page numbers in **bold type** refer to illustrations and captions.

Alexander the Great 29, 30
Alkibiades 13, 19
altars 10, **10**, 17, **17**
Altis, the 7, 10, 11, 15, 16, 17, 19, 25
Apollo, god 10, **28**
Atalanta, woman hero **4**, 27, **27**
Athena, goddess **5**, 18, **28, 29**
Athens 13, 31, **31**

Berlin, Germany **31**
boxing 11, 20, 22, **22**, 23, **23**
boys' contests 11

chariot races **4**, **5**, **9**, 12-13, **12**, **13**, 29
cheating **11**, 13, 14, 17, 23, **23**
Corinth **28**
Coubertin, Baron Pierre de 31, **31**

Delphi **28**
diaulos 18
discus 14, **14**
dolikhos 17, **17**

Elis 6, 8, **31**

funeral games **4**, 5, 18

gods 5, 9, 11
gymnasium 6, 7

health and cleanliness 7, **7**
Hera, goddess 26
  temple of 11, 26, **26**
Herakles (and the 12 Labours) 5, **5**, 10, 11, 21, **21**, 28

heralds 8
Hermes, god **7**, 10
heroes **4**, 5, 11, 21
Hill of Kronos **4**, 30
hippodrome 12-13, **12**
hoplitodromos 23, **23**
horse races and jockeys 13, **13**, 29
Isthmian Games 28, **28**, 29, 29

javelins **4**, 14-15, **14**, **15**
judges 6, 7, 10, 11, **11**, 16, 25, 29

Kleitomakhos, wrestler 21
Koroibos, athlete 5
Kronos **4**, 5

Leonidas, athlete 19
long jump 15, **15**

marathon 17
medals **24**, 25
modern Olympics 31, **31**

nakedness of competitors 7, 17, 26
Nemean Games 28, **28**, 29
Nike, goddess **25**

oath 6, 10, **11**, 13
Olympic flame **11**, **28**
Olympic symbol **11**
Owens, Jesse **31**

palaistra 6, **6**, 7, **7**
Panathenaic Games **28**, 29, **29**
panhellenic games 28-9
pankration 20, 23, **23**
Patroklos, hero **4**, 18

Peleus, hero 21, **27**
Pelops, hero 5, 11, 12, 15
pentathlon 14-15
politics **31**
prizes **4**, **24**, 29
professional athletes 29
public banquet 16, 19, 25
Pythian Games 28, **28**, 29

runners 17, 18-19

sacrifices 5, 10, 16, 17, **17**, 19
seating 9, **9**, 12
Sostratos, pankratiast 23
Sparta, Spartans 9, **26**, 27, **31**
sprint races 5, 15, 18, 26
stade (short sprint) 5, 18
starting line and starting positions 19, **19**, **31**
swimming 7

Telemakhos, wrestler 21
temples 11, 16, **16**, 25, **27**, 27
trainers and training 6-7, **21**, **23**, 26
triple jump 15

victory procession 25, **25**

warriors 14, 23, 27
winners 24-5
women competitors **5**, 15, 26-7, 31
wreaths 8, 25, 26, **29**
wrestling 5, 6, **6**, 11, 15, 20, **20**, 21, **21**, 23
Zeus, king of the gods 4, 5, 9, 10, 11, 16-17, **28**, 30
Zeus' statue 11, **11**, 17
Zeus' temple 11, **16**, 17, 23, 25